in
the
news™

THE GREAT HOPE FOR AN ENERGY ALTERNATIVE

Laser-Powered Fusion Energy

Carol Hand

ROSEN
PUBLISHING®

New York

To Dale-Marie—cheerleader, contact, and friend

Published in 2011 by The Rosen Publishing Group, Inc.
29 East 21st Street, New York, NY 10010

Library of Congress Cataloging-in-Publication Data

Hand, Carol.
The great hope for an energy alternative : laser-powered fusion energy/Carol Hand. — 1st ed.
    p. cm. (In the News)
Includes bibliographical references and index.
ISBN 978-1-4358-9450-1 (library binding) —
ISBN 978-1-4488-1682-8 (pbk.) —
ISBN 978-1-4488-1690-3 (6-pack)
1. Laser fusion—Juvenile literature. I. Title.
QC791.775.L37H36 2011
621.48'4—dc22

                                                    2009052258

Manufactured in the United States of America

CPSIA Compliance Information: Batch #S10YA: For further information, contact Rosen Publishing, New York, New York, at 1-800-237-9932.

On the cover: Top left: The National Ignition Facility visitor center. Top right: The NIF main amplifiers provide 99.9 percent of the NIF's energy. Bottom: An artist's rendering of an NIF target pellet inside a hohlraum capsule.

contents

The Promise of Nuclear Energy

For many years, people have been searching for an "ultimate" energy source. This means a limitless, or sustainable, source—one that will never run out. It should also have few or no side effects. It should not cause human health problems, damage the environment, or change the climate.

An experimental and potentially limitless energy source may generate most of our future electricity. It is a form of nuclear energy called laser-powered fusion, laser-induced fusion, or just laser fusion. But why do we need a new energy source? What's wrong with today's sources? What exactly is nuclear energy? Is it safe? Is it really limitless? And specifically, what is laser fusion and why is it so promising?

The Sun: Source of All Energy

Without energy from the sun, Earth would be a rocky, barren planet with no light, no warmth, and certainly no life. Fossil fuels (coal, oil, and natural gas) are the remains of ancient plants, which captured and stored the sun's energy. That energy, stored several hundred million years ago, is now being released by fossil fuel burning.

The sun is also the source of alternative forms of energy. Solar power relies on the direct capture of the sun's energy by focusing it onto solar panels or cells. Windmills capture wind currents driven around Earth by the sun's energy. Now crops are grown just

The Luminant Lake Hubbard natural gas power plant is located in Dallas, Texas.

to burn them for energy production. This biomass energy is an updated form of fossil fuel energy. It uses present-day, rather than ancient, plants as fuel. And one form of nuclear energy—nuclear fusion—produces energy using exactly the same chemical reaction as the sun.

The Decline of Fossil Fuels

Over the past two hundred years, humans have become extremely dependent on coal, oil, and natural gas. Many people cannot imagine living without them. But these fossil fuels are definitely not the ultimate energy source.

Firstly, they are limited, or nonrenewable. People must constantly locate and mine new fossil fuel deposits. As fossil fuels are burned, new sources become harder to find. Secondly, fossil fuels are major polluters. Mining them damages and sometimes destroys land and ocean ecosystems. Burning them releases particles and gases into the air. This produces smog and other highly toxic air pollution, which causes serious health problems.

Finally, burning coal, oil, and—to a lesser extent—natural gas releases greenhouse gases. These gases enter the upper atmosphere, trap the sun's heat, and radiate it back to Earth's surface. The atmosphere naturally contains tiny amounts of greenhouse gases. They keep Earth warm and filled with life. But even a small increase in greenhouse gases causes too much heat to be trapped and Earth's temperature to rise. This global warming is happening as we burn more and more fossil fuels. (Fossil fuel burning is not the only factor causing Earth's temperature to rise. The climate is now in a natural warming cycle. But Earth is heating much faster than normal, due partly to fossil fuel burning.)

For these reasons, many people feel we must find replacements for fossil fuels. They think we can no longer afford to depend on this destructive source. Alternative energy sources all show promise, and some are beginning to be used on a large scale. But they cannot produce the large amounts of continuous energy needed to replace fossil fuels. Nuclear energy might provide this.

What Is Nuclear Energy?

Nuclear energy is energy contained in the nuclei of atoms. Albert Einstein's equation, $E = mc^2$, taught that it was possible to capture and use this type of energy. This equation says mass can be converted into energy, and vice versa. In fact, because c^2 (the speed of light squared) is a very, very large number, the

Smog over the Los Angeles skyline illustrates a major disadvantage of fossil fuel energy.

equation says a very tiny amount of mass can be converted into a very large amount of energy. But to be usable, the energy confined in atomic nuclei must be released. This can happen in three ways: radioactive decay, nuclear fission, and nuclear fusion. All of these are exothermic reactions—that is, they release energy.

Radioactive Decay

Radioactive decay occurs naturally. A radioactive, or unstable, form of an atom spontaneously decays, or emits particles. This transforms it into another kind of atom with a lower energy level. A radioactive atom goes

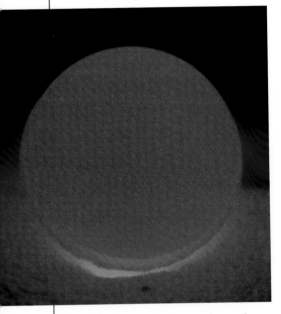

Plutonium is highly toxic and carcinogenic (cancer-causing). This pellet is glowing with its own radioactivity.

through a series of decay until it reaches a stable state. Each element decays at a specific rate. This rate is defined by the element's half-life, or the time it takes for one-half of the atoms in any sample to decay. The radioactive element plutonium-239 has a half-life of 24,065 years. Deuterium, or "heavy hydrogen," has a half-life of 12.35 years.

Radioactive decay cannot provide energy for human civilization. It occurs much too slowly and on too small a scale. It does not produce the huge amounts of energy we require.

Nuclear Fission

In nuclear fission, a large or "heavy" atomic nucleus splits apart to form two smaller or "lighter" nuclei. Splitting the nucleus causes an explosion of energy. The first large-scale use of nuclear fission was the atomic bomb. In 1945, atomic bombs were dropped on two Japanese cities, Hiroshima and Nagasaki. The devastation was so great that it led to the end of World War II. An atomic bomb is an uncontrolled fission reaction. To be used as an energy source, fission must be controlled.

Controlled fission is the only form of nuclear energy currently used as a power source. Commercial fission reactors use two major fuels, uranium-235 (^{235}U) and plutonium-239 (^{239}Pu). Products from splitting these fuels are highly radioactive. Some have very long half-lives. They must be stored for thousands of years until natural radioactive decay returns them to a safe, stable form. For this reason, many people object to using nuclear fission as a power source. They wonder where the waste can be safely stored.

Nuclear Fusion

In nuclear fusion, two small ("light") atomic nuclei fuse together at very high temperatures and pressures. This forms one larger nucleus. For example, two forms of heavy hydrogen (deuterium, ^{2}H, and tritium, ^{3}H) can fuse to form a single helium atom (^{4}He). Fusion releases even more energy than fission. The sun uses this reaction to produce heat and light energy.

An uncontrolled fusion reaction produces a hydrogen bomb. To control the reaction, it must be slowed. Small packets of fuel must be fed in to produce short, continuous bursts of energy. To get fusion started, a tremendous amount of energy must be put into the

An engineer works on radioactive fuels at the Cadarache Nuclear Research Center in France.

reaction—enough to overcome the forces that want to keep fusion from happening. Finally, a controlled fusion reaction must be rapid and sustained to produce a continuous supply of energy. A fusion power plant would require five to ten fusion reactions per second. In short, to make fusion a usable energy source, we must build a baby sun—or many of them—right here on Earth.

Our Nuclear Future

Both fission and fusion may have their place in our future energy picture. Currently, there is pressure to jump-start the nuclear fission industry. Some people want to build new power plants and upgrade existing ones. Also, scientists are exploring better ways to handle nuclear waste. Instead of long-term storage, they hope to reprocess decay products and reuse them as fuel sources. This would make fission more sustainable and radioactive storage leaks less likely.

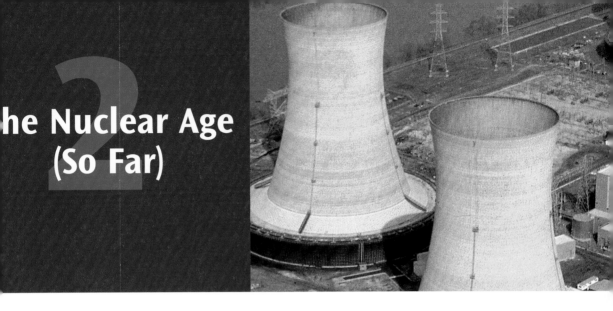

It is much easier to split one large atom into two than to fuse two small atoms. So the dawn of atomic (nuclear) energy began with fission, not fusion. As Adolf Hitler was coming to power in Germany during the 1930s, scientists in Britain, America, and Germany were discovering how to split uranium atoms—the first nuclear fission reactions. They quickly realized fission's potential as a weapon. In 1939, Albert Einstein wrote a letter to the U.S. president, Franklin D. Roosevelt, warning him of uranium's potential. Einstein feared the Germans would make a bomb and use it against the United States and other countries.

The Atomic (Fission) Bomb

When the United States entered World War II in 1941, work on the atomic bomb was already under way. At the University of Chicago, Enrico Fermi and Leo Szilard built the first "atomic pile" (a fifty-seven-layer stack consisting of tons of uranium oxide sandwiched between graphite blocks). The bomb project, named the Manhattan Project, was moved to Los Alamos, New Mexico, for secrecy. Led by physicist J. Robert Oppenheimer, a group of about one hundred scientists spent three years building and testing the first atomic bombs. Many of them were refugees from Hitler's Germany, and many would win Nobel Prizes.

Dr. Glenn T. Seaborg, a Nobel Prize–winning chemist, discovered ten atomic elements, including plutonium.

The Hydrogen (Fusion) Bomb

Even before the first atomic bombs were dropped, scientists were working on the hydrogen bomb, which was powered by fusion. The United States exploded the first hydrogen bomb in the South Pacific in 1952. It completely destroyed an island on Eniwetok Atoll. It left a giant crater and produced a mushroom cloud 20 miles (32 kilometers) high and 100 miles (161 km) wide. It was seven hundred times larger than the atomic bomb dropped on Hiroshima.

Even scientists who helped develop atomic weapons were horrified by their destructive power. Some, such as Danish physicist Niels Bohr, wanted all countries to know atomic weapon secrets. Bohr felt this would prevent any one country from stockpiling weapons and could even end war. Others, including Oppenheimer and Fermi, completely opposed further development of the hydrogen bomb on moral grounds. But Edward Teller, another giant of the Manhattan Project and a fanatical anti-communist, lobbied strongly for a full-scale fusion program. He wanted to develop more and bigger bombs to pro-tect us from a Soviet

J. Robert Oppenheimer, head of the Manhattan Project, later worked to limit nuclear weapons.

attack. Teller's group won. The arms race between the United States and the Soviet Union, called the Cold War, lasted more than forty years.

Besides the obvious threat of nuclear war, every nuclear explosion releases a cloud of radiation, or radioactive fallout. Some types of fallout are deadly. In the 1950s, scientists realized levels of radioactive stron-tium-90 (^{90}Sr) from fission bombs were building up around the world and becoming a serious health hazard. These threats led to a series of test-ban treaties to regulate nuclear weapon testing.

Fission Reactors

After World War II, countries began to develop nuclear fission power plants to produce electricity. People thought nuclear power would provide very inexpensive energy—energy that was "too cheap to meter." Also, Western countries were beginning to import oil. They hoped nuclear power would replace fossil fuels, reducing our dependence on oil from the Middle East.

But producing electricity was more difficult than making a bomb. Controlled nuclear reactions heat water to produce steam, which is then used to generate electricity. This requires a critical mass of fuel—a large enough amount of either uranium-235 or plutonium-239 to initiate the reaction. As the first uranium atoms split, they start a chain reaction. Neutrons released from each splitting atom smash into more and more atoms, splitting them in turn. This chain reaction continues until the fuel runs out. In a bomb, all of the heat and light energy is released at once in a giant explosion. In a power plant, the chain reaction must be slowed down, or moderated, so the energy is released gradually. All U.S. fission reactors are "light water" reactors, which use regular water as a moderator.

Electric Power from Nuclear Fission

In 1956, the first commercial fission reactor was opened at Calder Hall, in the United Kingdom. In 1958, the first commercial U.S. nuclear plant, the Shippingport plant in Pennsylvania, went online.

For about twenty years, the U.S. nuclear power industry surged. But enthusiasm for nuclear energy waned quickly. The promised inexpensive energy never happened. Plants were costly to build and had to compete with fossil-fuel plants. Then, in 1979, a cooling unit

The Three Mile Island nuclear power plant accident decreased confidence in the U.S. nuclear power industry.

malfunctioned in a reactor at Pennsylvania's Three Mile Island nuclear power plant. The coolant drained away, the reactor core heated up, and a partial meltdown occurred. It destroyed the reactor and released radioactive gas into the atmosphere. Luckily, no injuries resulted. But this accident increased the public's fears about nuclear power. At one time, there were orders for 259 nuclear reactors, but more than 100 were eventually cancelled. By 2007, the United States had only 104 reactors operating.

Current and Future Fission

Today, nuclear fission reactors provide about 15 percent of the world's electrical energy. Fossil fuels provide about 65 percent. According to the World Nuclear Association (WNA), the world's demand for electricity will double by 2030, due to population growth and increased standards of living. The WNA feels fission power plants can solve this need for energy. Uranium supplies are abundant. Compared to fossil fuels, nuclear fuel produces the same amount of energy using much less fuel. This makes fuel storage and transport easier. Fission energy is becoming more affordable as coal and oil prices rise. Finally, the WNA says that, because nuclear fission energy does not release carbon dioxide, it does not contribute to global warming.

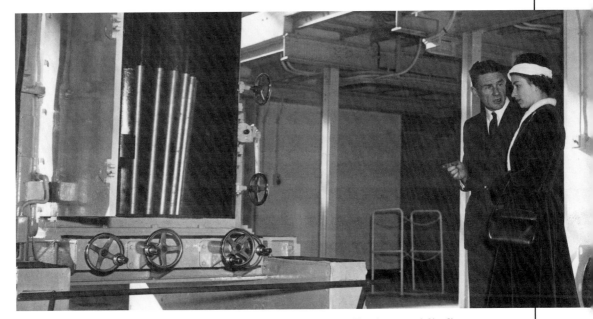

Queen Elizabeth II attends the opening of Calder Hall, the world's first commercial fission reactor.

Not everyone is so optimistic about nuclear fission energy. Many U.S. citizens still resist its use. They worry about safe long-term storage of dangerous nuclear waste and the possibility of more accidents like that at Three Mile Island. People also fear nuclear fuel meant for power plants could be stolen and used by terrorists to build nuclear weapons. And studies show fission does contribute to global warming. More fission reactors will probably be built in the United States, but building them will likely cause controversy.

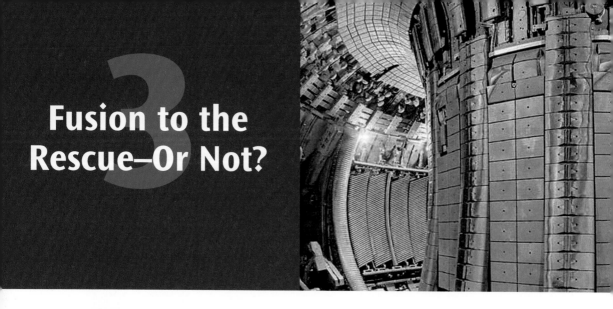

Fusion to the Rescue—Or Not?

Fission and fusion both result from energy changes in the nuclei of atoms. Fission reactions happen spontaneously during radioactive decay, but there is nothing spontaneous about a fusion reaction. Fusion happens only under extreme conditions, like those in the sun. Matter on Earth is typically solid, liquid, or gas. But for fusion to occur, matter must be transformed into a fourth state called plasma. Plasma is so hot and so compressed that electrons are stripped from the nuclei of its atoms. The electrons and nuclei mingle freely as electrically charged particles, or ions. Vast amounts of fuel and intense gravity create these conditions in the sun. It's not so easy to create them on Earth.

The Road to Fusion

For more than sixty years, scientists have explored ways to start and sustain fusion reactions. Progress has been slow. Some people declared success too soon or even faked results. In 1951, Ronald Richter, a little-known scientist in Argentina, claimed he had fused deuterium and lithium at the very low temperature of 10,000 degrees Fahrenheit (5,538 degrees Celsius). Scientists were highly skeptical. They knew from bomb tests that fusion occurred only at millions of degrees, when matter became plasma. Richter was discredited—tests of his "reactor" showed no radiation at all. Fusion was not occurring.

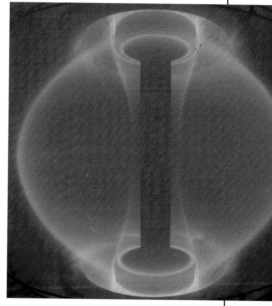

Inside a tokamak, fusion reactions reach temperatures of 180 million°F (100 million°C).

But Richter's claims made other scientists consider how to contain a controlled fusion reaction. They realized magnetic fields strongly affect ions in plasma, and several designs were developed using this concept. Promising designs came from Princeton University, Los Alamos National Laboratory, and the United Kingdom. This led Indian physicist Homi Bhabha to state in 1955 that "a method will be found for liberating fusion-energy in a controlled manner within the next two decades. When that happens, the energy problems of the world will truly have been solved." Bhabha spoke far too soon. But in 1969, a Russian design called the tokamak proved much more efficient than earlier devices. It is still the major container used in magnetic fusion research.

In 1962, only two years after discovery of the laser, physicists at Lawrence Livermore National Laboratory proposed the use of laser beams to initiate fusion reactions. This began the concept of inertial confinement fusion systems, now one of the most promising fusion systems.

Some people tried shortcuts to fusion. One of the most outrageous attempts was the "cold fusion" fiasco of 1989. Two respected chemists working at the University of Utah claimed they had produced sustained fusion at room temperature. Martin Fleischmann and B. Stanley Pons performed electrolysis of heavy water (containing the heavy hydrogen atom, deuterium) using an electrode of the metal palladium. They claimed their tabletop system was producing heat and huge numbers of neutrons—both evidence of a sustained fusion reaction.

However, Pons and Fleischmann announced their results at a press conference, rather than publishing a paper. They provided no actual data and no description of their methods. So other scientists could not repeat their experiments and test their results. When the truth finally came out, it was clear fusion was not occurring. Most people felt the scientists had actually faked results. Some people still do cold fusion research. But to avoid

B. Stanley Pons *(left)* and Martin Fleischmann defend cold fusion before a House committee in 1989.

the taint of the Pons-Fleischmann study, they describe their work as low energy nuclear reaction (LENR) studies, not cold fusion.

What Is a Fusion Reaction?

The most common fusion fuels are hydrogen isotopes. An isotope is an alternative form of an atom. It has the same number of protons but a different number of neutrons in its nucleus. The nucleus of a typical hydrogen atom contains only one particle—a positive proton. Deuterium has two particles in its nucleus—one proton and one neutron. Tritium has one proton and two neutrons. The reaction using these two "heavy hydrogen" isotopes is called the D-T reaction.

A single D-T reaction looks like this:

$$^2D + {}^3T \rightarrow {}^4He \text{ (3.5 MeV)} + n \text{ (14.1 MeV)}$$

In this reaction, one deuterium atom and one tritium atom fuse to form one helium atom. In the process, one neutron is released. The small numbers in front of each atom show the number of particles in its nucleus. The values 3.5 and 14.1 are measures of the energy released in this reaction. The energy unit "MeV" means "mega electron volt." When fusion occurs, a very small amount of deuterium and tritium—say, the amount in a pinhead—releases about as much energy as the amount in a gallon of gasoline. This means a fusion reaction releases about a million times more energy than a chemical reaction.

Two Ways to Start Fusion

Scientists are pursuing two general methods for containing and igniting the reaction: magnetic confinement and inertial confinement.

The tokamak of the Joint European Torus (JET) facility in Culham, England, is the world's largest fusion device.

In magnetic confinement, hundreds of cubic meters of fuel are enclosed in a tokamak. This is a magnetic torus, or doughnut-shaped structure with an electrical current running through its center. It compresses and heats the fuel to 18 million°F (10 million°C), forming plasma. Ions in the plasma follow magnetic field lines, so they flow around the torus and stay confined within it. As the temperature and pressure increase, the rapidly moving protons collide and fuse. This is presently the most effective magnetic confinement system. Two other magnetic confinement systems, stellarators and reversed field pitch (RFP) systems, have different arrangements of their magnetic fields.

In the second process, inertial confinement, a tiny D-T fuel pellet is bombarded with a laser beam, an ion beam, or X-rays. The beam heats the outer skin of the fuel pellet. The outer layer explodes, causing an inward reactive force, or implosion. This both heats and compresses the pellet's interior, starting fusion. The released energy explodes outward, causing more fusion and starting a chain reaction. Inertial fusion uses pulsed energy beams to maintain the reaction. The pulses are extremely short (less than one billionth of a second) and each pulse compresses the fuel to a density much greater than that of lead. Laser fusion is one form of inertial confinement fusion.

The Basic Laser Fusion Reactor

The core of a laser-powered fusion reactor contains the fuel—a deuterium-tritium mixture. A 3.3-foot-thick (1-meter-thick) "blanket" of lithium surrounds the core. When fuel in the core is heated enough, fusion begins, releasing heat and neutrons. The lithium absorbs and slows down the neutrons. In the process, lithium is transformed into helium and tritium. The tritium becomes more fuel for the reactor. Water flowing through the lithium blanket picks up the heat, cooling the reactor. The super-heated water forms steam, which is used to generate electricity.

Sounds easy, doesn't it? But it is extremely difficult to achieve ignition—that is, to get the fusion reaction going. Fusing two nuclei requires pushing their protons together until they stick. But protons are positively charged, and positive charges repel each other. They must be forced together. To do this, the fuel must be heated until it becomes plasma and contained long enough for fusion to begin—and continue. Until enough energy is generated by the fusion reactions to overcome the amount put in to ignite the reaction, there is no net gain from fusion. That is, there is no energy left over to generate electricity.

Fusion Projects

No one knows whether magnetic or inertial confinement systems will be more practical, so test facilities are studying both. Eventually, there may be both types of commercial fusion reactors, just as there are now several types of fission reactors.

So far, magnetic confinement has been studied more than inertial confinement. Several important tokamaks have been built around the world. The Tokamak Fusion Test Reactor (TFTR) at Princeton University in New

The largest U.S. fusion test occurred at Princeton University's Tokamak Fusion Test Reactor (TFTR).

Jersey ran from 1982 to 1997. It was the first fusion reactor to test plasmas produced with D-T fuel. It produced a plasma temperature of 918 million°F (510 million°C), a record for that time. The Joint European Torus (JET) in the UK is still operating. It first produced plasma in 1983. In 1991, it was the first reactor to produce controlled fusion power. JET also pioneered the use of remote handling techniques to maintain the reactor interior, an important safety feature. Japan and Korea are operating similar tokamaks. The world's largest stellarator, the

Large Helical Device (LHD), is located in Japan. It has been operating since 1998.

The newest and best hope for solving the problems of magnetic confinement is the ITER (pronounced "eater") facility in Cadarache, France. ITER (International Thermonuclear Experimental Reactor) began construction in 2006. Its tokamak begins experiments in 2014. It is a collaboration of many countries—the European Union, Russia, the United States, Japan, South Korea, and China. ITER is gigantic. Its reactor magnet weighs 925 tons! If successful, it will generate 400 megawatts of energy for up to 500 seconds. This would be a major breakthrough, both in amount of energy produced and time the reaction is sustained.

Also, several important laser fusion facilities have recently started. One is the National Ignition Facility (NIF) in California. Another, called the Laser Mégajoule (LMJ), is in Bordeaux, France. Both facilities were built to support military applications. However, their findings will also help develop commercial fusion reactors. Information from these projects will lay the groundwork for more advanced laser fusion projects, including PETAL and HiPER, already under way in Europe.

The NIF Project

The first step in building a fusion power plant is to light the fusion fire—or, in scientific terms, achieve fusion ignition and energy gain. After fusion starts, it must burn hot enough and long enough to exceed the break-even point. This is the point where the amount of energy produced equals the amount used to start the reaction. All energy produced after the break-even point is energy gain. In a commercial fusion power plant, the energy gain would be used to generate electricity.

In the NIF project, lasers light and sustain the fusion fire. They cause fuel pellets to reach extreme conditions of heat and pressure even greater than those inside the sun. The NIF project will be the first in the world to demonstrate both fusion ignition and energy gain.

The National Ignition Facility (NIF)

The National Ignition Facility is located at the Lawrence Livermore National Laboratory in Livermore, California.

Laser Bay 2 contains half of the NIF's 192 lasers, which bombard a tiny fuel target to initiate fusion.

It opened on March 30, 2009. Many U.S. government agencies, universities, and industries are collaborating on this project.

Fusion reactions take place in a building the size of three football fields. Two separate bays house 192 laser units. The target chamber is shielded with concrete. It is about 33 feet (10 meters) in diameter and weighs around 1 million pounds (454 metric tons). In the exact center of the target chamber is a pellet of D-T fuel smaller than a pea. The pellet is inside a tiny, dime-sized gold cylinder, or hohlraum. *Hohlraum* is German for "cavity", or hollow area. Huge, specially coated mirrors are mounted on ten-story-tall structures at both ends of the laser bays. Four-foot-thick (1.2-meter-thick) concrete walls anchor these structures, making them extremely stable. The 192 laser beams bounce from mirror to mirror, boosting their energy content as they go.

Laser operation must be incredibly precise. Each pulse of laser light lasts only one-billionth of a second and travels 328 feet (100 m) to reach the tiny fuel pellet. Each beam must focus directly on the pellet, and all beams must reach it at exactly the same time. Large, sophisticated computers coordinate the system's thousands of mirrors, lenses, lasers, and diagnostic tools. The NIF scientists compare this precision to "standing on the pitcher's mound at AT&T Park in San Francisco and throwing a strike at Dodger Stadium in Los Angeles, some 350 miles [563 km] away."

Everything inside the NIF must be extremely clean. No piece of debris, dust, or oil can touch the lasers or mirrors during either construction or operation. The tiniest bit of dirt can damage the optics. The entire facility is kept cleaner than factories that manufacture electronic components or drugs for human use.

The NIF Laser System

Laser means "light amplification by stimulated emission of radiation." To amplify light means to make it stronger or more intense—that is, to increase its energy content.

"Stimulated emission of radiation" means to add energy to a special type of matter until it reaches a higher energy level and begins to emit photons, or packets of light. The photons emitted by a laser all have the same wavelength (the same amount of energy). They are also "coherent" (the peaks and troughs of all photon waves occur at the same time). So a laser beam—such as a laser pointer—is focused, straight, and bright. In contrast, ordinary light has many wavelengths and is not coherent. It tends to diffuse, or spread out. For example, a flashlight beam widens and dims as it gets farther away. Certain types of gases, crystals, and glass can be used as lasers. The first laser was made from ruby. NIF lasers are a special type of phosphate glass. These types of lasers, made from solid matter, are called solid-state lasers.

NIF Lasers

The NIF lasers emit photons in bursts, or pulses. The amplifiers of the NIF system contain 3,070 slabs of laser glass, each about 3 feet (0.9 meter) long and 1.5 feet (0.5 meter) wide. They are infused with atoms of the element neodymium, a soft metal that gives the glass a pinkish or reddish color. The slabs are bathed with bright, white light from 7,500 giant flashlamps. This energizes the neodymium atoms. When a weak laser pulse passes through the glass, these atoms release their extra energy. The laser beam picks it up and becomes brighter.

A scientist watches the growth of a ruby crystal. The first laser, demonstrated in 1960, was made of ruby.

Amping Up the Energy

The laser beam begins in the master oscillator as infrared rays. At this point, it has a tiny energy content—only one-billionth of a joule. It zooms through two systems of laser glass amplifiers bathed with light. First, it splits into forty-eight parts and travels through pream- plifiers. This amplifies it ten billion times, to a total energy of several joules. Then, each of the 48 beams splits into 4 parts, mak- ing 192 separate beams. Each beam first enters the power amplifier and then zips back and forth through the laser glass slabs in the main amplifier cavity. After leaving the main amplifier cavity, each laser beam holds 20,000 joules of energy.

These energized laser beams enter two complex sys- tems of mirrors, called switchyards. The switchyards bend the light from straight, parallel rays into a spheri- cal set of beams. This focuses them on the target fuel pellet. But before entering the target chamber, they pass through a final set of lenses. Here, they are converted to high-energy ultraviolet (UV) rays.

The hohlraum containing the fuel pellet is open at both ends. The UV laser beams stream through these openings. The hohlraum walls absorb and reradiate the energy as X-rays, which are even more energetic than UV rays. This process evenly distributes the laser beam energy so that it radiates toward the fuel pellet equally from all directions. This ensures that the fuel pellet and hohlraum compress evenly during the fusion reaction.

As the hohlraum and fuel pellet absorb the greatly amplified energy, they heat and compress until they far exceed conditions inside the sun. Their temperatures reach 180 million°F (100 million°C). Pressures are one hundred billion times greater than Earth's atmospheric pressure. They become one hundred times denser than lead. At these extreme conditions, plasma forms, the fuel ignites, and fusion begins. The fusion reaction spreads quickly through the fuel. It fuses to become helium, releasing its stored energy as heat.

The End Result

It takes a long time to explain the laser's path. But the beams travel at the speed of light. A laser beam takes only about five-millionths of a second to travel from its origin to the target 328 feet (100 m) away. But during this

Mark Jackson gives a tour of the new National Ignition Facility (NIF) in Livermore, California.

time, its energy increases from one-billionth of a joule to almost 4 million joules. That's an energy boost of more than a quadrillion (a thousand trillion) times!

NIF lasers focus at least sixty times more energy on the tiny fuel target than any previous laser system has produced. If experiments go as expected, the resulting fusion reaction will demonstrate an energy gain of twenty to fifty times more energy than the amount injected by the laser. One drawback of the NIF is that it can run only a few experiments per day because the optics must cool between runs. This problem will be addressed in other facilities, such as the European HiPER.

NIF's Goals

The NIF just began operation in 2009, but its list of projects will easily run for thirty years. A major goal is to demonstrate both fusion ignition and energy gain. This is the first step in developing a workable fusion power plant. Another goal involves national security. The NIF projects will help the military maintain the safety and reliability of thermonuclear weapons.

To help understand fusion reactions, the NIF will also explore basic science. Its experiments are opening up a whole new field called high energy density (HED) science. Scientists will observe changes in material properties under extreme conditions. They will generate detailed X-ray photographs of the inside of targets to show physical changes during fusion reactions. They will study astrophysics in the laboratory, since the NIF reactions are the same as those in stars. They will study plasma physics, optical physics, radiation sources, and properties of radiation. This basic science knowledge is exciting by itself. It will also contribute to many practical applications—including the development of fusion power.

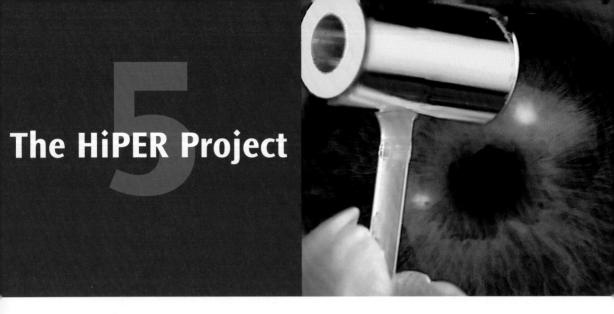

The HiPER Project

Both the NIF project in California and the Laser Mégajoule (LMJ) facility near Bordeaux, France, use the central ignition process to initiate fusion. Both facilities will demonstrate use of a high-powered laser to start and briefly sustain a fusion reaction and achieve energy gain. This is the first step toward building a commercial fusion reactor.

The European HiPER (High Power laser Energy Research) project will take the next step. They will use a more efficient ignition method called fast ignition. HiPER's planning and design phase runs through 2011, followed by a five-year building phase. It should begin operation in the early 2020s. The United Kingdom (UK) is taking the lead, but five other European countries (France, Greece, Italy, Spain, and the Czech Republic) are full partners. In all, HiPER directly involves twenty-five institutions from eleven countries. Plus, the United States, Canada, Japan, China, Russia, and the Republic of Korea are sharing research from their facilities. HiPER

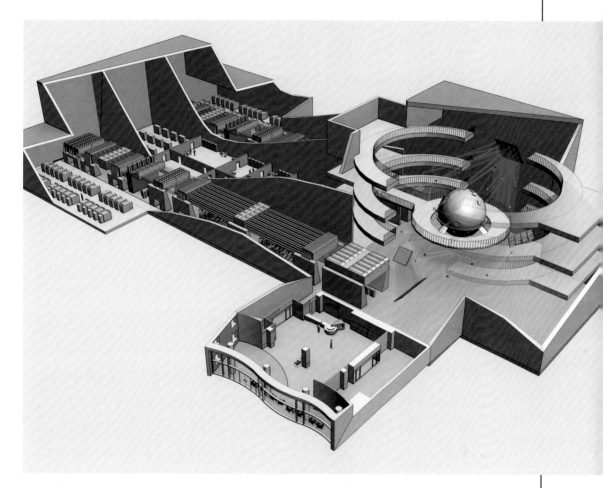

The HiPER (High Power laser Energy Research) facility, a European cooperative venture, will pioneer fast ignition fusion.

planners are studying all these research results to help determine HiPER's exact design and the direction its research will take.

France plays a key role in the HiPER partnership. Their new PETAL facility, near the LMJ in Bordeaux, is beginning to investigate fast ignition. Their results will feed directly into HiPER's planning and design stages. Like NIF and LMJ, the PETAL and HiPER facilities will become world-class research centers for the basic sciences behind nuclear fusion, particularly high energy density (HED) sciences. Unlike earlier facilities, they will focus on civilian, not military, uses.

Central Ignition vs. Fast Ignition

The NIF and HiPER projects use different types of laser fusion. The processes, called central ignition and fast ignition, differ in the way lasers are used to ignite fusion reactions.

Professor Mike Dunne, head of the Central Laser Facility at the Rutherford Appleton Laboratory in the UK, is the HiPER project director. Dunne compares central ignition (used at NIF and LMJ) to starting a diesel engine. No spark plugs are used. Diesel fuel is simply compressed until it ignites. In central ignition laser fusion, the fuel pellet is heated and compressed at the same time. When the amplified laser beam enters and bounces around inside the hohlraum, it transforms into X-rays. The extreme temperature and pressure implodes (compresses) the hohlraum and causes fuel ignition. This method is called indirect drive because the X-rays inside the hohlraum, rather than the laser itself, drive ignition.

Central ignition requires a large, powerful laser to achieve an extremely high temperature and pressure. The laser beams must deliver megajoules of energy and must be operated with pinpoint accuracy. X-rays must bathe the fuel pellet evenly from all sides. Also, the fuel pellet and hohlraum must be extremely symmetrical. The slightest roughness or variation in shape causes instabilities that slow compression and prevent ignition. Overall, central ignition

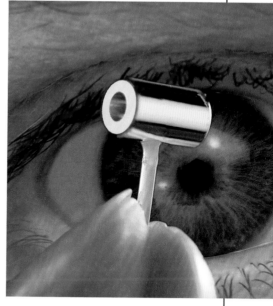

The hohlraum contains the fuel capsule and must be completely symmetrical so that laser beams bathe the fuel evenly.

is difficult, expensive, and not very efficient. The amount of energy produced in the NIF and LMJ will range from ten to thirty or even fifty times more than the break-even amount. This shows that energy production using laser fusion is possible. But running a commercial fusion power plant requires a more efficient process.

Professor Dunne says fast ignition may be that process. It is similar to a gasoline engine, where fuel heating and compression occur separately. The gasoline is compressed by pistons and heated to ignition by a spark plug. Fast ignition uses direct drive, in which lasers directly cause ignition. First, a small laser compresses the D-T fuel. Then, a second, more powerful laser (the "spark plug") ignites the fusion reaction. It heats a small spot on the fuel pellet using a series of very rapid pulses.

The fast ignition approach has several advantages. Less fuel compression means a much smaller laser is required. Instead of a laser delivering megajoules of energy, the direct drive method requires only kilojoules. Also, the target fuel pellet does not require such exact symmetry or need to be heated uniformly. So the fast ignition laser system is both less expensive and more efficient. A laser only one-fifth as large as a central ignition system laser could increase energy efficiency ten times. The energy gain could be nearly one hundred times the break-even amount, rather than only ten to fifty times.

Achieving HiPER Fusion

HiPER scientists hope to optimize the fast ignition process. But first, they must solve several major technological problems. HiPER research will center on the heating phase of the reaction. Researchers will study the physics required to generate, transport, and deliver energy to the fuel pellet. This process uses a laser that produces a high-energy beam of electrons or protons. The beam must deposit its energy into the already compressed fuel target and raise its temperature high enough to initiate fusion. In one target design, the laser is fired into the tip of a gold cone, producing hot electrons. The fuel compresses around the cone. As the laser beam passes through the cone, it is separated from the plasma. It can travel more freely and raise the fuel temperature higher.

HiPER scientists must also design a laser that fires pulses with a high repetition rate (rep-rate). Rapid, almost continuous pulses—at least five to ten per second—will be required for commercial fusion power plants. The HiPER test facility will explore at least two approaches for increasing rep-rates. The first would improve on the process used by the NIF and LMJ. This low-risk approach would achieve rep-rates of only about one per hour. The second approach is newer and less tested, but it would achieve rep-rates of about one per second. If successful, this would be an important technological breakthrough.

Working Up to HiPER

Several academic facilities already operating in the European Union are supplying their data and experience to prepare for the HiPER project. One of these is Vulcan, at the Central Laser Facility of the Rutherford Appleton Laboratory in the UK. This is currently the world's most powerful laser system.

Also, several medium-sized laser facilities have recently upgraded from central ignition to fast ignition lasers. The upgrades involve the addition of very high-energy lasers required for the heating phase of fast ignition. Results of their research will be used to improve the HiPER design.

One of these facilities is PETAL, associated with the LMJ near Bordeaux. PETAL is short for "Petawatt Aquitaine Laser." Aquitaine refers to the region of France where the facility is located. Petawatt is a measure of power. One petawatt equals 10^{15} (one quadrillion, or 1,000,000,000,000,000) watts. In contrast, today's U.S. fission reactors produce from 500 to 1,200 megawatts. A megawatt is 10^6 (one million, or 1,000,000) watts. Both PETAL and HiPER will generate power in the petawatt range—that is, about a billion times more energy than current fission reactors.

PETAL's compression laser will be part of the laser system from the adjacent LMJ facility. A second, stronger laser will heat the compressed fuel pellet with a laser pulse of up to 3.5 kilojoules (3,500 joules) for 0.5 to 5 trillionths of a second. Planning for the PETAL project began in 2005. Its first experiments will run from 2010 to 2013.

The Future of Fusion

Where does humanity now stand in its attempt to harness fusion power? Since research began in the 1950s, there have been many false starts and a few complete fiascos. It seems fusion power is always just around the corner. But scientists worldwide are still optimistic. Breakthroughs have been made, and they are confident technological problems can be solved. Many tentatively predict that a commercial fusion plant could be online by about 2050.

But researchers are not putting all their fusion eggs in one basket. They continue to explore both major fusion options—magnetic confinement and inertial confinement, or laser-powered fusion. The NIF and LMJ facilities, followed by HiPER and its many supporting facilities, are tackling the problems with laser fusion. Magnetic confinement research will be led by the ITER facility in Cadarache, France.

The Goal: An IFE Power Plant

The ultimate goal of inertial confinement facilities is to develop commercial fusion power plants fired by lasers. Like today's coal- or fission-powered plants, they would produce electricity for homes, schools, businesses, and factories. Laser fusion scientists have made general blueprints showing what a working IFE (inertial fusion energy) power plant would look like. It would include a target factory producing fuel pellets, a multibeam driver laser, a fusion chamber where the reaction occurs, and a turbine generator that receives the heat generated by fusion and turns it into electricity.

Target Factory

The target factory produces many tiny, low-cost fuel targets. Each target is a packet of D-T fuel inside a spherical capsule, probably made of a carbon-hydrogen polymer. Targets are injected from the target factory into the fusion chamber at speeds of more than 300 feet (91 m) per second. Several types of injectors are being tested, including gas guns and electromagnetic accelerators. The target factory must produce at least four hundred thousand targets per day.

Driver Laser

In direct-drive (fast ignition) fusion, the driver laser beams must send five to ten pulses of energy per second to the fuel target to maintain constant fusion. The laser must sustain these very high rep-rates without damaging the system. It must be efficient, low-cost, and very reliable. At least two types of lasers are being considered— solid-state lasers and krypton-fluoride gas lasers.

Fusion Chamber

As each target achieves fusion, it releases a burst of very high-energy neutrons, X-rays, and ions. The fusion chamber's inner

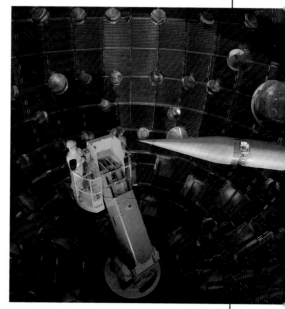

Inside the NIF target chamber, the tiny pencil-shaped object *(right)* holds the fuel pellet. A service module carries technicians.

wall must withstand this blast of energy. Any fusion chamber must contain a 20- to 40-inch-thick (50 to 100 centimeters) liquid lithium blanket, or "breeding blanket." The lithium would react with the released neutrons to generate, or "breed," tritium, which adds fuel for the D-T reaction. It might also serve as the inner wall of the chamber. This design is called a thick liquid wall.

Conditions inside the fusion chamber must be able to recover between laser pulses. Otherwise, fusion will not occur. This becomes harder as the number of pulses increases. At the NIF, only a few pulses per day can be generated. At HiPER, the goal is one pulse per second.

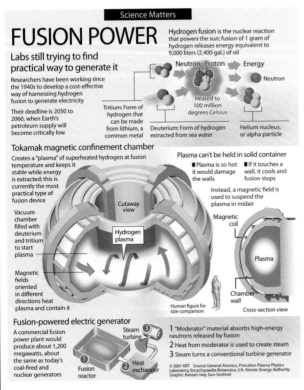

Science Matters

FUSION POWER

Labs still trying to find practical way to generate it

Researchers have been working since the 1940s to develop a cost-effective way of harnessing hydrogen fusion to generate electricity.

Their deadline is 2050 to 2060, when Earth's petroleum supply will become critically low

Hydrogen fusion is the nuclear reaction that powers the sun; fusion of 1 gram of hydrogen releases energy equivalent to 9,000 liters (2,400 gal.) of oil

Neutron Proton   Energy

Neutron

Heated to 100 million degrees Celsius

Tritium: Form of hydrogen that can be made from lithium, a common metal

Deuterium: Form of hydrogen extracted from sea water

Helium nucleus, or alpha particle

Tokamak magnetic confinement chamber

Creates a "plasma" of superheated hydrogen at fusion temperature and keeps it stable while energy is extracted; this is currently the most practical type of fusion device

Vacuum chamber filled with deuterium and tritium to start plasma

Magnetic fields oriented in different directions heat plasma and contain it

Cutaway view

Hydrogen plasma

Plasma can't be held in solid container

■ Plasma is so hot it would damage the walls

■ If it touches a wall, it cools and fusion stops

Instead, a magnetic field is used to suspend the plasma in midair

Magnetic coil

Plasma

Human figure for size comparison

Chamber wall

Cross-section view

Fusion-powered electric generator

A commercial fusion power plant would produce about 1,200 megawatts, about the same as today's coal-fired and nuclear generators

Steam turbine

Fusion reactor

Heat exchanger

1 "Moderator" material absorbs high-energy neutrons released by fusion

2 Heat from moderator is used to create steam

3 Steam turns a conventional turbine generator

© 2001 KRT Source: General Atomics, Princeton Plasma Physics Laboratory, Encyclopaedia Britannica, U.K. Atomic Energy Authority Graphic: Karsten Ivey, Sun-Sentinel

New research projects, such as the NIF and HiPER, are bringing fusion power into the media spotlight.

This is a tremendous improvement, but still below the five to ten required for commercial use.

Power Conversion System

The power conversion system removes the heat generated in the chamber. A coolant flows through the chamber walls at a constant rate. It absorbs the heat generated by the pulsed fusion reactions and delivers it to the turbine generator. The generator converts the heat to electricity. If lithium is used in the breeding blanket to produce tritium, it is also used as the coolant.

Is Fusion the Ultimate Energy Source?

Fusion might be one long-term solution to Earth's power needs. It may be the closest to an "ultimate" energy source anyone has so far imagined. But we are not there yet. Fusion reactors will not contribute electricity to the world power grid until at least 2050. It will take that long for projects such as the NIF and HiPER to solve major technological problems. Then companies must build commercial fusion plants. Fusion has much to recommend it. But every energy source comes with a cost. No source is free and no source is totally clean—including fusion.

Ice cubes made of deuterium oxide, or heavy water, sink *(left)*; those made of regular water float *(right)*.

Abundant and Available

Fossil fuels are nonrenewable and are being depleted. We are using them more rapidly as the population and energy demand grow. There may only be enough oil for the next 40 to 50 years and enough coal for 250 to 500 years. As supplies decrease, they become more expensive and harder to obtain. New technologies and discovery of new deposits may prolong supplies. But climate change may still dictate that we rely less and less on fossil fuels. Fission may replace or supplement fossil fuel power for a while. Uranium is much more plentiful than fossil fuels, but it will also eventually run out.

But every gallon of seawater contains enough deuterium to produce energy equivalent to 300 gallons (113 dekaliters) of gasoline. A single cubic kilometer of seawater contains deuterium equivalent to the world's entire oil reserves. Tritium is radioactive and does not occur naturally, but it can be made inside laser fusion reactors from lithium. Lithium is found in Earth's crust, in some soils, and (in small amounts) in seawater. So the fuels needed for D-T fusion are cheaper than either uranium or fossil fuels. Plus, everyone can obtain them without depending on foreign countries, which might raise prices or become enemies. Scientists hope the second generation of fusion reactors will use a D-D reaction. This would remove the need for tritium, making fuel even cheaper and more abundant. There is enough fusion fuel to last millions of years.

Efficient and Productive

Fusion energy is efficient. That is, a very tiny amount of fuel produces a very large amount of energy. According to author Alfred W. Crosby, "A gram of hydrogen converted to helium releases about 100 million times as much energy as a gram of TNT and 8 times as much as a gram of uranium." This means both the cost of transporting fusion fuel and the amount stored at the reactor site will be very small. So fusion—if it becomes practical—will outshine both fossil fuels and fission as an energy source.

Also, although the major goal of fusion power is to produce heat to make electricity, it might have an important by-product. Some of the reactor's heat can be used to split the helium produced during fusion. This makes hydrogen, which can then be used in hydrogen fuel cells to power vehicles.

Carbon-Free but Not Heat-Free

Unlike fossil fuels, fission and fusion are both carbon-free energy sources. They do not release carbon dioxide or other greenhouse gases into the atmosphere. Coal-fired power plants now account for more than 80 percent of greenhouse gas emissions. Replacing coal-fired plants with either fission or fusion plants would remove this source of global warming.

However, nuclear power still contributes to global warming. No power plant is 100 percent efficient. That is, not all of its heat goes to produce electricity. Some (often much) of it is released directly into the atmosphere. Current fission plants produce three times as much heat as the energy of the electricity they generate. Fusion plants will likely release large amounts of heat, too. To prevent fusion from contributing to global warming, this heat must be captured so that it will not enter the atmosphere. The cycle converting helium to hydrogen is one possibility.

Safe but Not Completely Safe

A reactor meltdown (such as the one that happened at Three Mile Island) cannot happen in a fusion reactor. They use very small amounts of fuel, and when the reactor temperature decreases, fusion simply stops. Helium, the chief fusion by-product, can be safely released into the atmosphere. Small amounts of tritium (radioactive hydrogen) are also produced, but it has a short half-life (about twelve years) and does not build up in the human body. In contrast, the radioactive waste produced by fission power plants includes highly toxic compounds with very long half-lives. This waste must be stored securely where it will not threaten human lives for a very long time—about three hundred thousand years, according to the National Academy of Sciences.

Fusion is definitely the safer choice. But it is not com-pletely clean and safe. More than 70 percent of fusion products are neutrons. These billions of particles contin-uously smash into the reactor walls, making them radioactive. The amount of radioactivity absorbed depends on the type of container—metals, concrete, and lithium-lead cooling blankets absorb neutrons differently. Metal tokamak walls become highly radioactive, weak,

If fusion energy takes off, an important future career will be fusion reactor maintenance technician.

and brittle. The entire reactor chamber must then be replaced. Best estimates indicate most radioactivity in fusion chambers decays to safe levels within one hundred years.

So switching to fusion does not remove the problem of radioactive waste storage entirely. The waste is generated in a different way. With fission, the waste is spent fuel—that is, uranium or plutonium that has undergone fission and produced radioactive waste products. With fusion, the radioactive waste is not spent fuel, but the reactor itself. But because the waste is shorter-lived and less toxic than fission waste, storage poses a much smaller problem.

Fusion scientists are considering this problem. One solution is to separate the most radioactive reactor components. The safe components could then be reused and only a small amount of waste would be stored for long time periods. Also, they are searching for new metal alloys that will be less damaged by neutrons. However, these materials may be very expensive. At this time, the problem of neutron bombardment appears to be little studied in laser fusion systems. It may be that absorption of radiation by the thick liquid wall of lithium, which can be periodically replaced, will be a solution.

What's Taking So Long?

Laser fusion advocates are understandably excited about the potential for this power source. But they are also realistic. They know fusion will be an important power source if it can be made practical—but can it? There are still tremendous hurdles to overcome and many years of research ahead. Hurdles include, but are not limited to, the creation of the following:

- A laser system capable of generating five to ten pulses per second and delivering them at speeds fast enough to trigger fusion reactions

- A target chamber whose materials can withstand and contain fusion reactions reaching millions of degrees without breaking down or becoming dangerously radioactive
- A target fuel pellet that can survive rapid-fire injection into the target chamber and undergo fusion when bombarded by a laser pulse
- A fast, accurate method for fuel-pellet injection
- Ways to capture waste heat so it will not contribute to global warming

If all of these problems can be solved in the timeline scientists now predict, fusion power could be a reality by about 2050. Of course, no one can predict the future. But physicist Daniel Goodstein has said, "No matter what else happens, this is the century in which we must learn to live without fossil fuels." Many people agree with him. And if this is the case, the strong, international effort currently under way to achieve fusion power may be one solution.

But even if fusion seems to be the ultimate energy source, it will still be only one of many sources used to meet world energy demands. Fossil fuel and fission energy will be around for decades, even generations. Energy conservation and efficiency will be increasingly important. Alternative energy sources will dominate in certain geographic regions. In short, future citizens of Earth will likely have many "eggs" — including laser fusion — in their energy "basket."

Glossary

central ignition Igniting a fusion reaction by compressing and heating the entire fuel pellet simultaneously with very strong lasers.

chain reaction A continuous reaction such as that created when atoms are split and release neutrons, which are then absorbed by other atoms, causing them to split.

critical mass The amount of nuclear fuel needed to initiate a nuclear reaction.

deuterium A form of heavy hydrogen containing two nuclear particles (one proton and one neutron); the major fuel in D-T fusion reactions.

fast ignition Igniting a fusion reaction by separately compressing and heating the fuel.

half-life The time required for one-half of the atoms in any radioactive sample to decay to a non-radioactive state.

hohlraum A dime-sized cylinder surrounding a fusion fuel pellet made of heavy metals (often gold) with holes on either end for the laser beam to pass through.

ignition The process of heating and compressing a nuclear fuel pellet until a chain reaction begins and the fusion process becomes self-sustaining.

isotope A different form of an atom having the same number of protons but a different number of neutrons in its nucleus.

laser A type of gas, crystal, or glass that can greatly amplify light, forming a high-energy coherent beam of a single wavelength; short for "light amplification by stimulated emission of radiation."

lithium The lightest metallic element, used as a "blanket" to absorb heat from the fusion chamber; it also generates tritium for use as a fusion fuel.

neodymium A soft metallic element with atomic number 60; used in laser glass to amplify the laser beam.

nuclear fission The release of energy as heat and light caused by breaking apart a large ("heavy") atomic nucleus to form two smaller ("lighter") nuclei.

nuclear fusion The release of energy as heat and light caused by fusing two or more small ("light") atomic nuclei to form one larger ("heavier") nucleus.

plasma The fourth state of matter so hot and compressed that electrons are stripped from atomic nuclei and mingle freely; for example, matter in the sun.

tokamak A doughnut-shaped magnetic chamber used to confine a fusion reaction; typically used in magnetic confinement fusion.

tritium A radioactive form of heavy hydrogen containing three nuclear particles (one proton and two neutrons); one of the fuels in the D-T fusion reaction.

For More Information

Canadian Nuclear Society
480 University Avenue
Suite 200
Toronto, ON M5G 1V2
Canada
(416) 977-7620
Web site:
http://www.cns-snc.ca/branches/Toronto/fusion/index.html
This site contains general information about fusion, plus descriptions of fusion research in Canada and around the world. The information is fairly technical.

Energy Information Administration (EIA)
1000 Independence Avenue SW
Washington, DC 20585
(202) 586-8800
Web site: http://www.eia.doe.gov/kids
This site, sponsored by the U.S. Department of Energy, has a kids' page with facts on different types of energy, a history of energy, games and activities, and a glossary of energy terms.

General Fusion, Inc.
108—3680 Bonneville Place

Burnaby, BC V3N 4T5
Canada
(604) 439-3003
Web site: http://www.generalfusion.com
This small Canadian start-up company is pioneering a
new approach to fusion, the magnetized target fusion
(MTF) approach, which is midway between magnetic
fusion and inertial confinement fusion. Its Web site
explains the process, plus gives general information on
the need for renewable energy and on the fusion process.

HiPER (High Power laser Energy Research Facility)
Central Laser Facility
Rutherford Appleton Laboratory
Chilton, Didcot
Oxfordshire, OX11 0QX
UK
Web site: http://www.hiper-laser.org
This site gives detailed information on the HiPER proj-
ect, the fast ignition laser fusion facility that will be the
successor to the NIF. It describes the project and gives
basic information on fusion.

National Ignition Facility & Photon Society (NIF)
Lawrence Livermore National Laboratory
7000 East Avenue
Livermore, CA 94550

Web site: https://lasers.llnl.gov
The National Ignition Facility & Photon Society is the foremost laser fusion facility in the United States. This site contains general information about fusion, specific information about the NIF project, and an education section with information and activities for all ages.

U.S. Department of Energy
1000 Independence Avenue SW
Washington, DC 20585
1-800-dial-DOE (342-5363)
Web site: http://www.ne.doe.gov/students/electra_energyfacts.html
The "Student Zone" of the U.S. Department of Energy's Web site has sections on energy facts, nuclear power plants, and careers, and contains a glossary. However, the entire site deals with fission, not fusion.

Web Sites

Due to the changing nature of Internet links, Rosen Publishing has developed an online list of Web sites related to the subject of this book. This site is updated regularly. Please use this link to access the list:

http://www.rosenlinks.com/itn/lpfe

For Further Reading

Ballard, Carol. *From Steam Engines to Nuclear Fusion: Discovering Energy.* Mankato, MN: Heinemann-Raintree, 2007.

Billings, Charlene W., and John Tabak. *Lasers: The Technology and Uses of Crafted Light* (Science and Technology in Focus). New York, NY: Facts on File, 2006.

Haggis-on-Whey, Doris, and Benny Haggis-on-Whey. *Cold Fusion* (HOW). San Francisco, CA: McSweeney's, 2009.

Hakim, Joy. *The Story of Science: Einstein Adds a New Dimension.* Washington, DC/New York, NY: Smithsonian Books, 2007.

Klages, Ellen. *The Green Glass Sea.* New York, NY: Puffin, 2008.

Klages, Ellen. *White Sands, Red Menace.* New York, NY: Viking Juvenile, 2008.

Nardo, Don. *The Lucent Library of Science and Technology: Lasers.* 1st ed. San Diego, CA: Lucent Books, 2003.

Wyckoff, Edwin Brit. *Laser Man: Theodore H. Maiman and His Brilliant Invention* (Genius at Work! Great Inventor Biographies). Berkeley Heights, NJ: Enslow Elementary, 2007.

Yeatts, Tabatha. *Sterling Biographies: Albert Einstein: The Miracle Mind.* New York, NY: Sterling, 2007.

Bibliography

Boston University, Physics Department. "Radioactive Decay." 2000. Retrieved July 19, 2009. (http://physics.bu.edu/py106/notes/ RadioactiveDecay.html).

Crosby, Alfred W. *Children of the Sun: A History of Humanity's Unappeasable Appetite for Energy.* New York, NY: W. W. Norton & Company, 2006.

Dunne, M., et al. "HiPER Technical Background and Conceptual Design Report 2007." Retrieved September 27, 2009 (http://www.hiper-laser.org/overview/TDR/tdr.asp).

El-Guebaly, L. A., R. A. Forrest, T. D. Marshall, N. P. Taylor, K. Tobita, and M. Zucchetti. "Current Challenges Facing Recycling and Clearance of Fusion Radioactive Materials." Fusion Technology Institute, University of Wisconsin, November 2005. Retrieved October 3, 2009 (http://fti.neep.wisc.edu/pdf/fdm1285.pdf).

Energy Information Administration, Department of Energy. "History of Energy in the United States: 1635–2000." Retrieved August 29, 2009 (http://www.eia.doe.gov/emeu/aer/eh/frame.html).

FusEdWeb: Fusion Energy Education. "Plasmas—The Fourth State of Matter." Lawrence Livermore

National Laboratory and Princeton Plasma Physics Laboratory. Retrieved September 7, 2009 (http://fusedweb.llnl.gov/CPEP/Chart_Pages/5.Plasma 4StateMatter.html).

Hakim, Joy. *The Story of Science: Einstein Adds a New Dimension.* Washington, DC/New York, NY: Smithsonian Books, 2007.

HiPER Project. "HiPER: Laser Science for Our Future." 2009. Retrieved September 13, 2009 (http://www.hiper-laser.org/index.asp).

Lawrence Livermore National Laboratory. National Ignition Facility. "The National Ignition Facility: Ushering in a New Age for Science." 2009. Retrieved September 13, 2009 (https://lasers.llnl.gov/ programs/nif).

Nave, Carl R. HyperPhysics, Georgia State University. "Light Water Reactors." 2006. Retrieved September 6, 2009 (http://hyperphysics.phyastr.gsu.edu/Hbase/ nucene/ligwat.html#c1).

Nordell, Bo, and Bruno Gervet. "Global Energy Accumulation and Net Heat Emission." *International Journal of Global Warming*, 2009, Vol. 1, No. 1/2/3, pp. 378-391. Quoted in: "Trapping Carbon Dioxide or Switching to Nuclear Power Not Enough to Solve Global Warming Problem, Experts Say." 2009. Retrieved October 6, 2009 (http://www.sciencedaily. com/releases/2009/07/090713085248.htm).

PETAL—PETawatt Aquataine Laser. "A Petawatt Laser Coupled with Four Nanoseconds Lasers Beams, Located in Aquitaine (France)." 2009. Retrieved September 20, 2009 (http://petal.aquitaine.fr/spip.php?lang=en).

Power Engineering International. "HiPER Activity." 2008. Retrieved September 26, 2009 (http://www.neimagazine.com/story.asp?storyCode=2051538).

Sci-Tech Encyclopedia. "Deuterium." *McGraw-Hill Encyclopedia of Science and Technology*. 5th ed. McGraw-Hill Companies, Inc. Retrieved September 7, 2009(http://www.answers.com/library/Sci%252DTech+Encyclopedia-cid-85610).

Seife, Charles. *Sun in a Bottle: The Strange History of Fusion and the Science of Wishful Thinking.* London, England: Penguin Books, Ltd., 2008.

United Kingdom Atomic Energy Authority. "Focus on Fusion." 2009. Retrieved August 29, 2009 (http://www.fusion.org.uk/focus/index.htm).

World Nuclear Association. "Chernobyl Accident." April 2009. Retrieved September 5, 2009 (http://www.world-nuclear.org/info/inf36.html).

Index

About the Author

Carol Hand has a Ph.D. in zoology with a concentration in ecology/environmental science. For the past eleven years, she has written middle and high school science curricula for a nationally known education company. She has also taught college and written for standardized testing companies. In her study of environmental science, she has had a special interest in alternative forms of energy, including fusion.

Photo Credits

Cover, pp. 29, 36, 39, 45 credit is given to Lawrence Livermore National Security, LLC, Lawrence Livermore National Laboratory, and the Department of Energy under whose auspices this work was performed; pp. 4, 8 U.S. Department of Energy/Photo Researchers, Inc.; p. 5 Bloomberg via Getty Images; p. 7 David McNew/Getty Images; p. 10 Anne-Christine Poujoulat/AFP/Getty Images; pp. 11, 15 Bill Pierce/Time & Life Pictures/Getty Images; pp. 12, 34 © AP Images; p. 13 Hulton Archive/Getty Images; p. 17 George W. Hales/Hulton Archive/Getty Images; pp. 18, 23 AFP/Getty Images; p. 19 Photoshot/Newscom; p. 21 Diana Walker/Time & Life Pictures/Getty Images; p. 26 pttmedical/Newscom; pp. 28, 32 Photoshot/Hulton Archive/Getty Images; p. 37 © 2010 HiPER Project (http://www.hiper-laser.org/pressandpr/imagegallery.asp); pp. 43, 47 Charles D. Winters/Photo Researchers, Inc.; p. 46 KRT/Newscom; p. 51 Maximilian Stock Ltd/Photo Researchers, Inc.

Designer: Tom Forget; Editor: Bethany Bryan;
Photo Researcher: Peter Tomlinson